# I Care for Nature

Katie Peters

GRL Consultants,
Diane Craig and Monica Marx,
Certified Literacy Specialists

Pull Ahead Readers People Smarts

Lerner Publications ◆ Minneapolis

**Note from a GRL Consultant**
This Pull Ahead leveled book has been carefully designed for beginning readers. A team of guided reading literacy experts has reviewed and leveled the book to ensure readers pull ahead and experience success.



Lerner Publications
An imprint of Lerner Publishing Group, Inc.
241 First Avenue North
Minneapolis, MN 55401 USA

For reading levels and more information, look up this title at www.lernerbooks.com.

Main body text set in Memphis Pro 24/39
Typeface provided by Linotype.

Photo Acknowledgments
The images in this book are used with the permission of: © BraunS/Getty Images, pp. 12–13; © fstop123/Getty Images, pp. 14–15, 16 (left); © LightFieldStudios/Getty Images, pp. 4–5, 16 (right); © MNStudio/Shutterstock Images, pp. 6–7; © poco_bw/Getty Images, pp. 8–9, 16 (center); © Wand_Prapan/Getty Images, pp. 10–11; © Waridsara_HappyChildren/Shutterstock Images, p. 3.

Front cover: © tratong/Shutterstock Images.

**Library of Congress Cataloging-in-Publication Data**

Names: Peters, Katie, author.
Title: I care for nature / Katie Peters.
Description: Minneapolis : Lerner Publications, [2023] | Series: I care (pull ahead readers people smarts - nonfiction) | Audience: Ages 4–7 | Audience: Grades K–1 | Summary: "Lakes, trees, and birds are all part of nature. Early readers can explore ways to care for nature in this easily accessible text. Pairs with the fiction book, Nature Walk"— Provided by publisher.
Identifiers: LCCN 2021045317 (print) | LCCN 2021045318 (ebook) | ISBN 9781728457642 (library binding) | ISBN 9781728461557 (ebook)
Subjects: LCSH: Nature—Juvenile literature.
Classification: LCC QH48 .P5227 2022 (print) | LCC QH48 (ebook) | DDC 508—dc23/eng/20211020

LC record available at https://lccn.loc.gov/2021045317
LC ebook record available at https://lccn.loc.gov/2021045318

Manufactured in the United States of America
1 – CG – 7/15/22

# Table of Contents

# I Care for Nature

Trees are part of nature.

I can help plant a tree.

Birds are part of nature.

I can help feed the birds.

Flowers are part of nature.
I can help water the flowers.

Lakes are part of nature.
I can help clean the shore.

Parks are part of nature.
I can follow the park rules.

I like to take care of nature.

## What do you like about nature?

## Did You See It?

carrots

flowers

tree

## Index